A Cast Iron Cookbook

A Cast Iron Skillet Book Filled With Delicious Cast Iron Recipes

By
BookSumo Press
All rights reserved

Published by
http://www.booksumo.com

ENJOY THE RECIPES?
KEEP ON COOKING WITH 6 MORE FREE COOKBOOKS!

Click the link below and simply enter your email address to join the club and receive your 6 cookbooks.

http://booksumo.com/magnet

https://www.instagram.com/booksumopress/

https://www.facebook.com/booksumo/

LEGAL NOTES

All Rights Reserved. No Part Of This Book May Be Reproduced Or Transmitted In Any Form Or By Any Means. Photocopying, Posting Online, And / Or Digital Copying Is Strictly Prohibited Unless Written Permission Is Granted By The Book's Publishing Company. Limited Use Of The Book's Text Is Permitted For Use In Reviews Written For The Public.

Table of Contents

Page	Recipe
5	Mexican Veggie Skillet
6	Tostadas
7	Catalina's Stir Fry
8	Tex Mex Breakfast Eggs
9	Tuesday's San Miguel Potatoes
10	Chicken Salad Phoenix Style
11	Traditional Mexican Spicy Vermicelli
12	A Tex-Mex Breakfast
13	San Antonio Stroganoff
14	Tex Mex Quesadillas x Fajitas
15	Shrimp w/ Jasmine Rice & Papaya
16	Ginger Chili Plum Steak
17	Jerk Stir-Fry
18	Vegetarian Sweet and Sour Stir Fry
19	Authentic Saag
20	Ginger Coconut Curry Chicken
21	Spicy Salmon Stir Fry
22	Ginger Coconut Curry Chicken
23	Simply Fried Bread
24	Spicy Skillet Broccoli
25	Mumbai Breakfast
26	Asian Apple Chicken Stir Fry
27	Steak Quesadillas
28	Thousand Island Beef Quesadillas
29	Vegetarian Quesadillas
30	Smoky Mushroom Quesadillas
31	Little Tike PB & J Quesadillas
32	Pear Fritters
33	Summer Pear Salad
34	Sweet and Sour Ground Beef
35	Tijuana Ground Beef
36	5-Ingredient Tomato Sauce
37	Traditional Mexican Tomato Sauce
38	Curry Chicken I
39	Skillet Marinara Sauce
40	Malaysian Mango Chicken
41	Vegetarian Mango Curry
42	Malaysian Mango Chicken
43	Hot Italian Skillet Pizza
44	Paella in Mediterranean Style
45	Argentinian Tomato & Corn Chicken
46	Louisiana Shrimp
47	American Fried Chicken Cutlets
48	Crispy Paprika Chicken
49	Apple & Cheddar Stuffed Chicken
50	Creamy Mushroom Skillet
51	Hearty Simple Burger
52	Fish and Chips
53	Szechwan Shrimp
54	Chicken Breasts With Chipotle Gravy
55	Banana & Brown Sugar Spring Rolls
56	Bed and Breakfast Pancakes
57	Skillet Buttery Bananas
58	Cabbage & Carrot Spring Rolls
59	Spicy Beef Spring Rolls
60	A Japanese Stir-Fry
61	The Best Chicken Stir-Fry I Know
62	Beef Stir-Fry I
63	Orange-Chicken Stir Fry
64	Turkey Stir-Fry
65	Tofu Stir Fry II
66	Chicken and Garlic
67	Lemon and Shrimp Stir Fry

Mexican Veggie Skillet

Prep Time: 20 mins
Total Time: 30 mins

Servings per Recipe: 4
Calories	212 kcal
Fat	4.6 g
Carbohydrates	36.8g
Protein	10.1 g
Cholesterol	0 mg
Sodium	818 mg

Ingredients

- 1 tbsp olive oil
- 1 large onion, chopped
- 3 cloves garlic, minced
- 4 small zucchini, diced
- 1 fresh poblano chili pepper, seeded and chopped
- 1 C. frozen whole kernel corn
- 1 (15 oz.) can black beans, rinsed and drained
- 1/2 tsp salt

Directions

1. In a large skillet, heat the oil on medium-high heat and sauté the onion and garlic till tender.
2. Add the zucchini and poblano pepper, and sauté till soft.
3. Stir in the corn and beans and cook till heated completely.
4. Season with the salt to taste

TOSTADAS

Prep Time: 10 mins
Total Time: 35 mins

Servings per Recipe: 8
Calories 402 kcal
Fat 20 g
Carbohydrates 20.5g
Protein 33.6 g
Cholesterol 91 mg
Sodium 395 mg

Ingredients

2 tbsp olive oil
1 large onion, cut into rings
1 (15 oz.) can stewed tomatoes
1 (7 oz.) can chipotle peppers in adobo sauce
2 lb. shredded cooked chicken meat
16 tostada shells
1/2 C. sour cream

Directions

1. In a pan, heat the oil on medium heat and sauté the onions for about 5 minutes.
2. Meanwhile, in a blender, add the tomatoes, chipotle peppers and adobo sauce and pulse till pureed.
3. Transfer the tomato mixture into the pan with the chicken.
4. Simmer, covered for about 20 minutes.
5. Place the chicken mixture onto tostada shells and top with a dollop of the sour cream.

Catalina's Stir Fry

Prep Time: 20 mins
Total Time: 35 mins

Servings per Recipe: 4
Calories	333 kcal
Fat	15.9 g
Carbohydrates	13.3g
Protein	32.1 g
Cholesterol	94 mg
Sodium	945 mg

Ingredients

1 tsp olive oil
1 green bell pepper, chopped
1 red bell pepper, chopped
2 tbsp all-purpose flour
1 (1 oz.) packet taco seasoning mix
1 lb. skinless, boneless chicken breast halves - cut into bite size pieces

2 tsp olive oil
1 (15 oz.) can black beans, rinsed and drained
1/2 C. prepared salsa
1 C. shredded Cheddar cheese

Directions

1. In a skillet, heat 1 tsp of the olive oil on medium-high heat and sauté the bell peppers for about 5 minutes.
2. Remove from the heat and keep aside.
3. In a bowl, mix together the flour and taco seasoning in a bowl.
4. Coat the chicken pieces with the flour mixture evenly.
5. In a large skillet, heat 2 tsp of the olive oil on medium-high heat and cook the chicken for about 5 minutes.
6. Stir in the bell peppers, black beans and salsa and simmer for about 5 minutes.
7. Serve with a sprinkling of the Cheddar cheese.

TEX MEX
Breakfast Eggs

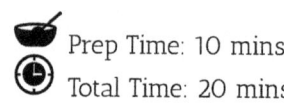

Prep Time: 10 mins
Total Time: 20 mins

Servings per Recipe: 6
Calories 283 kcal
Fat 12.2 g
Carbohydrates 30.8g
Protein 12.1 g
Cholesterol 196 mg
Sodium 661 mg

Ingredients

- 1 tbsp butter
- 1 (4 oz.) can chopped green chilis
- 1/2 tomato, chopped
- 6 large eggs
- 1/4 C. crushed tortilla chips
- 1/4 C. shredded sharp Cheddar cheese
- 6 (8 inch) flour tortillas
- 6 tbsp taco sauce

Directions

1. In a large skillet, melt the butter on medium heat and cook the green chilis and tomato for about 5 minutes.
2. Carefully, crack the eggs into the skillet and stir till the yolks break.
3. Cook, stirring for about 2-3 minutes.
4. Sprinkle the tortilla chips on top and mix with the eggs.
5. Move egg mixture to the side of the skillet and remove from the heat.
6. Immediately, sprinkle the Cheddar cheese over the egg mixture and keep aside, covered for about 5 minutes.
7. In a microwave-safe plate, place the flour tortillas and microwave for about 30 seconds.
8. Divide the egg mixture onto each tortilla and serve with a topping of the taco sauce.

Tuesday's San Miguel Potatoes

Prep Time: 10 mins
Total Time: 1 hr

Servings per Recipe: 4
Calories	420 kcal
Fat	13.2 g
Carbohydrates	60.3g
Protein	17.2 g
Cholesterol	25 mg
Sodium	681 mg

Ingredients

4 baking potatoes
1 tbsp vegetable oil
1 onion, chopped
1 large green bell pepper, chopped
1 tsp minced garlic
1 (16 oz.) can chili beans in spicy sauce, undrained
1 tbsp vegetarian Worcestershire sauce
1/2 tsp minced jalapeno peppers
1 C. shredded Monterey Jack cheese

Directions

1. With a sharp knife, scrub the potatoes and prick in several places.
2. Place the potatoes onto a paper towel and arrange in a microwave and microwave on high for about 8 minutes.
3. Turn and rotate the potatoes and microwave for about 8-10 minutes.
4. In a medium skillet, heat the oil on medium-high heat and sauté the onions and bell peppers till softened.
5. Stir in the beans, Worcestershire sauce, and jalapeño peppers.
6. Reduce the heat to low and simmer, covered for about 5-6 minutes.
7. Split the potatoes and top with the bean mixture.
8. Serve with a sprinkling of the cheese.

CHICKEN SALAD
Phoenix Style

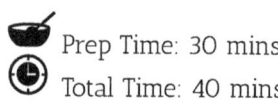
Prep Time: 30 mins
Total Time: 40 mins

Servings per Recipe: 2
Calories
Fat
Carbohydrates
Protein
Cholesterol
Sodium

Ingredients

1 whole skinless, boneless chicken breast, halved
2 tbsp Montreal steak seasoning
2 tbsp butter
1/2 head iceberg lettuce, chopped
1 tomato, chopped
1/2 green bell pepper, cut into 1/4-inch cubes
1/4 C. seeded and chopped jalapeno peppers, 3 tbsp juice reserved
2 tbsp chopped green chili peppers
1/4 C. drained canned corn kernels
1/4 C. drained sliced black olives
1/4 C. drained and rinsed black beans
1/2 C. shredded Cheddar-Monterey Jack cheese blend
1 C. ranch dressing
1/2 tsp ground black pepper
1/4 tsp garlic powder

Directions

1. Season the chicken breast with the Montreal steak seasoning evenly.
2. In a frying pan, melt the butter on medium heat and cook the chicken for about 5-10 minutes per side.
3. Remove the chicken from pan and cut into small pieces.
4. In a large bowl, add the lettuce, chicken, tomato, green bell pepper, jalapeño peppers, green chili peppers, corn, black olives, black beans and Cheddar-Monterey Jack cheese blend and gently toss to coat.
5. In another bowl, add the ranch dressing, reserved 3 tbsp of the jalapeño juice, black pepper and garlic powder and beat till well combed.
6. Place the dressing over the salad and toss to coat.

Traditional Mexican Spicy Vermicelli

Prep Time: 10 mins
Total Time: 35 mins

Servings per Recipe: 4
Calories	311.6
Fat	7.9g
Cholesterol	0.0mg
Sodium	891.6mg
Carbohydrates	51.7g
Protein	9.2g

Ingredients

- 2 tbsp vegetable oil
- 1 medium onion, chopped
- 2 garlic cloves, minced
- 8 oz. vermicelli, broken up, 2 C.
- 1 tsp salt
- 1/2 tsp pepper
- 1/2 tsp cumin
- 1 (4 oz.) cans green chilies, chopped
- 1 (8 oz.) cans tomato sauce
- 2 C. water

Directions

1. In a wide skillet, heat the oil on medium heat and cook the onion for about 10 minutes, stirring occasionally.
2. Add the garlic and cook for about 1-2 minutes.
3. Break the vermicelli into 2-inches pieces and add into the skillet.
4. Cook for about 3-4 minutes, stirring occasionally.
5. Add the salt, pepper, cumin, green chilies, tomato sauce and water and bring to a boil on high heat.
6. Reduce the heat to low and simmer, covered for about 10 minutes.

A TEX-MEX Breakfast

Prep Time: 15 mins
Total Time: 30 mins

Servings per Recipe: 4
Calories   413.7
Fat   33.4g
Cholesterol   230.5mg
Sodium   945.7mg
Carbohydrates   16.1g
Protein   13.3g

Ingredients

3 C. Simply Potatoes® Shredded Hash Browns
1/2 tsp salt
2 tsp cumin, divided
1/2 tsp chili powder
1/2 C. panko breadcrumbs
1/3 C. Mexican cheese, shredded blend
3 tbsp vegetable oil
1 tbsp butter

4 eggs
2/3 C. sour cream
2 tbsp cilantro
2 tbsp sun-dried tomatoes, chopped
3 scallions, finely chopped
1/2 C. salsa
4 slices turkey bacon, cooked

Directions

1. In a bowl, add the hash browns, salt, 1 tsp of the cumin, chili powder, panko and cheese and stir till well combined.
2. Divide the potato mixture into 4 portions.
3. In a large skillet, heat the oil on medium heat until hot and cook the potato stacks for about 3 minutes.
4. Carefully, flip the side and cook till golden from both sides.
5. Transfer the stacks into a dish and cover with a foil paper.
6. In a non-stick skillet, melt the butter on low heat.
7. Add the eggs, one at a time and cook for about 2-3 minutes.
8. Flip and cook till done completely.
9. Meanwhile in a small bowl, mix together the sour cream, cilantro, reserved cumin, tomatoes and the whites of the scallions.
10. Arrange 1 haystack on a small plate and top with an egg, followed by 2 tbsp of the salsa, a slice of bacon cut in half and crossed and a dollop of the sour cream.
11. Serve with a garnishing of the greens from the scallions.

San Antonio Stroganoff

Prep Time: 10 mins
Total Time: 30 mins

Servings per Recipe: 6
Calories   499.4
Fat   15.4g
Cholesterol   138.9mg
Sodium   691.4mg
Carbohydrates   54.9g
Protein   35.6g

Ingredients

12 oz. extra wide egg noodles
1 tbsp butter, tossed with cooked noodles
1 1/2 lbs extra lean ground beef
1/2 C. chopped onion
3 (10 oz.) cans rotel, the diced tomatoes with green chilies (undrained)
1 C. frozen corn, thawed
1/4 C. water
1 tsp ground cumin
1/2 tsp garlic powder
1/4-1/2 tsp cayenne pepper
1/2 tsp pepper
salt, to taste
1 C. reduced-fat sour cream
1/4 C. chopped fresh cilantro, for garnish

Directions

1. In large pan of the boiling water, prepare the egg noodles according to the package's directions.
2. Drain well and return to the pan and toss with the butter.
3. Cover the pan to keep.
4. Meanwhile, heat a large skillet on medium heat and cook the beef and onion till browned completely.
5. Drain the excess grease from the skillet.
6. Add the Rotel, corn, water, cumin, garlic powder, cayenne, pepper and salt and bring to a gentle simmer.
7. Cook for about 10 minutes.
8. Stir in the reduced-fat sour cream and stir to blend well.
9. Cook till heated completely.
10. Serve over the hot cooked noodles with a garnishing of the chopped cilantro.

TEX MEX
Quesadillas x Fajitas

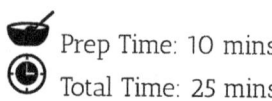

Prep Time: 10 mins
Total Time: 25 mins

Servings per Recipe: 4
Calories   552 kcal
Fat   31.1 g
Carbohydrates   40g
Protein   28 g
Cholesterol   79 mg
Sodium   859 mg

Ingredients

2 tbsp vegetable oil, divided
1/2 onion, sliced
1/2 green bell pepper, sliced
salt to taste
4 flour tortillas
1/2 lb. cooked steak, cut into 1/4-inch thick pieces
1 C. shredded Mexican cheese blend

Directions

1. In a 10-inch skillet, heat 2 tsp of the oil on medium heat and sauté the onion and green bell pepper for about 5-10 minutes.
2. Stir in the salt and transfer the mixture into a bowl.
3. Brush 1 side of each tortilla with the remaining oil.
4. In the same skillet, place 1 tortilla, oil-side down on medium heat.
5. Sprinkle with 1/2 of the steak, 1/2 of the onion mixture and 1/2 of the Mexican cheese mixture.
6. Place a second tortilla, oil-side up onto the cheese layer, pressing down with a spatula to seal.
7. Cook the quesadilla for about 3-4 minutes per side.
8. Remove the quesadilla from skillet and cut into wedges.
9. Repeat with the remaining ingredients for second quesadilla.

Saturday Night Spicy Shrimp with Jasmine Rice and Papaya

Prep Time: 30 mins
Total Time: 38 mins

Servings per Recipe: 4
Calories	903.1
Fat	3.8g
Cholesterol	0.0mg
Sodium	456.2mg
Carbohydrates	201.3g
Protein	14.4g

Ingredients

- 2 tsp canola oil, approximately
- 3 C. medium large frozen shrimp, peeled & deveined, thawed
- 2 C. fresh pineapple, peeled, and cut into large chunks
- 1 whole fresh papaya, peeled, halved and seeded, cut into large chunks
- 1 whole fresh mango, peeled, pit removed, and cut into chunks
- 1 1/3 C. orange juice, freshly squeezed
- 2-3 tsp lime juice
- 1/4 C. granulated sugar
- 3/4 tsp salt
- 1/4 C. white wine vinegar
- 4 tsp cornstarch
- 4 tbsp fresh flat leaf parsley, chopped, as garnish
- 4-6 C. cooked white jasmine rice, freshly cooked

Directions

1. In a bowl, add the vinegar and cornstarch and beat till smooth.
2. In a large skillet, heat the oil on medium-high heat and stir fry the shrimp for about 5 minutes.
3. With a slotted spoon, transfer the shrimp into a bowl and keep aside.
4. In the same skillet, stir together the orange juice, lime juice, sugar, pineapple, papaya and mango.
5. Add the cornstarch mixture, stirring continuously and bring to a boil.
6. Cook, stirring continuously for about 1 minute.
7. Add the shrimp and cook for about 1 minute stirring continuously.
8. Immediately remove from the heat.
9. Place the shrimp mixture over the hot cooked rice and serve with a garnishing of the parsley.

GINGER CHILI PLUM
Steak

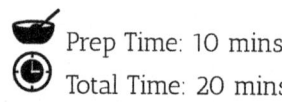

Prep Time: 10 mins
Total Time: 20 mins

Servings per Recipe: 4
Calories 550.3
Fat 30.3g
Cholesterol 140.7mg
Sodium 778.6mg
Carbohydrates 26.6g
Protein 40.1g

Ingredients

1.5 lbs rump steak
2/3 C. plum sauce
1 tbsp soy sauce
1 garlic clove, crushed
1 tsp fresh ginger, grated
1/2 tsp fresh red chili, chopped
2 tsp sugar
2 tsp dry sherry
2 tsp corn flour
2 tbsp oil
2 tsp corn flour, extra
½ C. water
1 small beef stock cube, crumbled

Directions

1. Trim the steak and slice thinly.
2. In a large bowl, mix together the steak slices, sauces, garlic, ginger, red chili, sugar, sherry and corn flour.
3. Refrigerate, covered to marinate for at least 30 minutes or overnight.
4. Remove the steak slices from the bowl and reserve the marinade.
5. In a wok, heat a little oil and stir fry the steak slices in batches till browned.
6. In a small bowl, dissolve the extra corn flour with water.
7. In the wok or skillet, add all steak slices, reserved marinade, corn flour mixture and stock cube and bring to a boil, stirring continuously.
8. Boil till the mixture thickens.
9. Serve with the rice.

Jerk Stir-Fry (Caribbean)

Prep Time: 15 mins
Total Time: 35 mins

Servings per Recipe: 2
Calories   549 kcal
Carbohydrates   41 g
Cholesterol   104 mg
Fat   21.4 g
Fiber   4.7 g
Protein   44.3 g
Sodium   1621 mg

Ingredients

- 1 tbsp vegetable oil
- 1 green bell pepper, seeded and cubed
- 1 red bell pepper, seeded and cubed
- 1/4 cup sliced sweet onions
- 3/4 pound skinless, boneless chicken breast, cut into strips
- 2 1/2 tsps Caribbean jerk seasoning
- 1/2 cup plum sauce
- 1 tbsp soy sauce
- 1/4 cup chopped roasted peanuts

Directions

1. Get wok or skillet, add oil, and for 7 mins stir fry your onions and peppers until they are soft. Once soft remove them from the pan.
2. Get a bowl and combine chicken and jerk seasoning. Evenly coat.
3. Stir fry chicken until cooked. Then add plum sauce and onions and peppers. Stir fry for five mins after chicken is cooked.
4. Add some soy sauce and peanuts.
5. Enjoy.
6. NOTE: Remember that all stir fries go great with rice.

VEGETARIAN SWEET and Sour Stir Fry

Prep Time: 10 mins
Total Time: 25 mins

Servings per Recipe: 2
Calories   377 kcal
Carbohydrates   35.3 g
Cholesterol   24.2 g
Fat   < 1 mg
Fiber   1.3 g
Protein   3.6 g
Sodium   3.6 g

Ingredients

1 (3.5 ounce) package ramen noodles (such as Nissin® Top Ramen)
3 tbsps olive oil
1 slice firm tofu, cubed
1/2 green bell pepper, chopped
1/4 small onion, chopped
1/3 cup plum sauce
1/3 cup sweet and sour sauce

Directions

1. Get a pan. Add water and salt. Heat until boiling.
2. Use the boiling water to cook your ramen noodles for three mins.
3. Get a wok, or skillet with medium heat get your olive oil hot.
4. Fry tofu, onions and pepper for 6 mins.
5. The tofu should be on one side of the pan, the onions on another side.
6. Combine the ramen with the tofu and peppers.
7. Mix in sweet and sour sauce and plum sauce.
8. Continue stir frying for three to five mins.
9. Let cool and enjoy.

Authentic Saag (Tasty Indian Spiced Mustard Greens and Spinach)

Prep Time: 30 mins
Total Time: 50 mins

Servings per Recipe: 6	
Calories	182 kcal
Fat	16.2 g
Carbohydrates	7.6 g
Protein	4.7 g
Cholesterol	41 mg
Sodium	565 mg

Ingredients

- 1/2 C. butter
- 2 tsp cumin seed
- 1 green chili pepper, seeded and diced
- 2 cloves garlic, chopped
- 2 tbsp ground turmeric
- 1 lb. chopped fresh mustard greens
- 1 lb. chopped fresh spinach
- 1 tsp ground cumin
- 1 tsp ground coriander
- 1 tsp salt

Directions

1. In a large skillet, melt the butter on medium-high heat and cook and sauté the cumin seed, chili pepper, garlic and turmeric for about 2 minutes.
2. Stir in the chopped mustard greens and spinach a little at a time, adding the stems and thicker leaves.
3. Slowly, add greens and cook till all the greens have been added and all are completely wilted.
4. Stir in the cumin, coriander, and salt.
5. Reduce the heat and simmer for about 10 minutes, adding water as needed to keep the greens moist.

GINGER COCONUT CURRY
Chicken

Prep Time: 20 mins
Total Time: 45 mins

Servings per Recipe: 4
Calories	313 kcal
Fat	21.7 g
Carbohydrates	14g
Protein	19.1 g
Cholesterol	38 mg
Sodium	268 mg

Ingredients

- 3 tbsp olive oil
- 1 small onion, chopped
- 2 cloves garlic, minced
- 3 tbsp curry powder
- 1 tsp ground cinnamon
- 1 tsp paprika
- 1 bay leaf
- 1/2 tsp grated fresh ginger root
- 1/2 tsp white sugar
- salt to taste
- 2 skinless, boneless chicken breast halves - cut into bite-size pieces
- 1 tbsp tomato paste
- 1 C. plain yogurt
- 3/4 C. coconut milk
- 1/2 lemon, juiced
- 1/2 tsp cayenne pepper

Directions

1. In a skillet, heat the olive oil on medium heat and sauté the onion till golden brown.
2. Stir in the garlic, curry powder, cinnamon, paprika, bay leaf, ginger, sugar and salt and sauté for about 2 minutes.
3. Add the chicken pieces, tomato paste, yogurt and coconut milk and bring to a boil.
4. Reduce the heat and simmer for about 20-25 minutes.
5. Discard the bay leaf and stir in the lemon juice and cayenne pepper.
6. Simmer for about 5 minutes.

Spicy Salmon Stir Fry

🥣 Prep Time: 20 mins
🕐 Total Time: 30 mins

Servings per Recipe: 2
Calories	765 kcal
Fat	47.1 g
Carbohydrates	11g
Protein	81.5 g
Cholesterol	1262 mg
Sodium	1783 mg

Ingredients

- 2 tbsp olive oil
- 3/4 tsp cumin seeds
- 1/2 tsp brown mustard seeds
- 1 small onion, sliced into thin half-circles
- 1 clove garlic, minced
- 1 tbsp minced fresh ginger root
- 1 green chili pepper, chopped
- 10 fresh curry leaves, chopped (optional)
- 1 tomato, diced
- 2 (14.75 oz.) cans salmon, drained and bones removed
- 1/4 C. chopped fresh cilantro

Directions

1. In a skillet, heat the oil on medium heat and sauté the cumin and mustard seeds till the seeds begin to pop.
2. Stir in the onions and sauté till golden brown.
3. Stir in the garlic, ginger, chili pepper and curry leaves and sauté till the garlic becomes golden.
4. Add the tomatoes and sauté for a few seconds.
5. Stir in the salmon and with the back of the stirring spoon, break the salmon into small pieces.
6. Cook for about 5-10 minutes.
7. Remove from the heat and serve with a garnishing of the cilantro.

GINGER COCONUT CURRY Chicken

🥣 Prep Time: 20 mins
🕐 Total Time: 45 mins

Servings per Recipe: 4
Calories   313 kcal
Fat   21.7 g
Carbohydrates   14g
Protein   19.1 g
Cholesterol   38 mg
Sodium   268 mg

Ingredients

3 tbsp olive oil
1 small onion, chopped
2 cloves garlic, minced
3 tbsp curry powder
1 tsp ground cinnamon
1 tsp paprika
1 bay leaf
1/2 tsp grated fresh ginger root
1/2 tsp white sugar

salt to taste
2 skinless, boneless chicken breast halves - cut into bite-size pieces
1 tbsp tomato paste
1 C. plain yogurt
3/4 C. coconut milk
1/2 lemon, juiced
1/2 tsp cayenne pepper

Directions

1. In a skillet, heat the olive oil on medium heat and sauté the onion till golden brown.
2. Stir in the garlic, curry powder, cinnamon, paprika, bay leaf, ginger, sugar and salt and sauté for about 2 minutes.
3. Add the chicken pieces, tomato paste, yogurt and coconut milk and bring to a boil.
4. Reduce the heat and simmer for about 20-25 minutes.
5. Discard the bay leaf and stir in the lemon juice and cayenne pepper.
6. Simmer for about 5 minutes.

Simply Fried Bread

Prep Time: 15 mins
Total Time: 25 mins

Servings per Recipe: 4
Calories   176 kcal
Fat   6.2 g
Carbohydrates   25.4 g
Protein   4.3 g
Cholesterol   1 mg
Sodium   271 mg

Ingredients

- 1 C. vegetable oil for frying, or as needed
- 1 C. unbleached flour
- 1 tsp baking powder
- 1 tsp powdered milk
- 1/4 tsp salt
- 1/2 C. water

Directions

1. In a heavy skillet, heat the oil to 350 degrees F.
2. In a large bowl, sift together the flour, baking powder, powdered milk and salt.
3. Place the water over the flour mixture and mix till a sticky dough forms.
4. With floured hands, make balls from the dough.
5. Fry the dough in the hot oil for about 3-4 minutes per side.
6. Transfer the fry bread to a paper towel-lined plate to drain

SPICY SKILLET
Broccoli

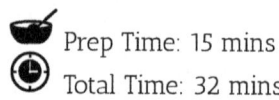
Prep Time: 15 mins
Total Time: 32 mins

Servings per Recipe: 4
Calories   164 kcal
Fat   12.3 g
Carbohydrates   10.2g
Protein   3.5 g
Cholesterol   0 mg
Sodium   1323 mg

Ingredients

3 tbsp vegetable oil
1/2 tsp mustard seed
1 small onion, chopped
1/2 tsp cumin seeds
1 tbsp ginger-garlic paste
1 tsp chili powder
1 tsp ground turmeric

1 head broccoli, chopped
2 tsp water
2 tsp salt
3 tbsp gram flour (garbanzo bean flour)
1 tsp vegetable oil

Directions

1. In a skillet, heat 3 tbsp of the oil on medium heat and sauté the mustard seeds for about 1-2 minutes.
2. Add the onion and cumin seeds and sauté for about 5-10 minutes.
3. Add the ginger-garlic paste, chili powder and turmeric and sauté for about 1-2 minutes.
4. Add the broccoli and cook for about 8-10 minutes.
5. Stir in the water and salt and cook for about 1 minute.
6. Add the gram flour and cook, stirring continuously for about 5-8 minutes.
7. Drizzle 1 tsp of the oil over junka and serve.

Mumbai Breakfast

Prep Time: 10 mins
Total Time: 15 mins

Servings per Recipe: 2
Calories   377 kcal
Fat   35.5 g
Carbohydrates   4g
Protein   12.3 g
Cholesterol   286 mg
Sodium   203 mg

Ingredients

1 tsp oil, or as needed
2 medium eggs
1/2 C. heavy whipping cream
1/4 clove garlic, minced
1/4 C. shredded Cheddar cheese, or more to taste
2 tsp curry powder
1 tsp ground cumin (optional)

Directions

1. In a skillet, heat the oil on medium-high heat.
2. In a bowl, add the eggs and cream and beat well.
3. Add the garlic, Cheddar cheese, curry powder and cumin and stir to combine.
4. Add the egg mixture in the hot oil and cook, stirring for about 5 minutes.

ASIAN APPLE CHICKEN Stir Fry

🥣 Prep Time: 15 mins
🕐 Total Time: 45 mins

Servings per Recipe: 4
Calories	305 kcal
Fat	11.6 g
Carbohydrates	19.6 g
Protein	30.6 g
Cholesterol	76 mg
Sodium	181 mg

Ingredients

- 2 tbsp olive oil
- 4 skinless, boneless chicken breast halves - cut into strips
- 1 large sweet onion, diced
- 2 Granny Smith apples - peeled, cored and sliced
- 1 red bell pepper, seeded and sliced into strips
- 1 tbsp red curry paste
- 1 tsp ground cinnamon
- 1/2 C. chicken broth
- 1 C. plain yogurt
- salt and pepper to taste

Directions

1. In a large skillet, heat the oil on medium-high heat and stir fry the chicken for about 5-10 minutes.
2. Transfer the chicken into a plate and keep aside.
3. In the same skillet, add the onion and apple on medium heat and sauté for about 8 minutes.
4. Add the bell pepper and cook and cook for about 5 minutes.
5. Stir in the curry paste and cinnamon and cook for a few more minutes.
6. Stir in the chicken broth, yogurt and cooked chicken and simmer for a few minutes till heated completely.
7. Remove from the heat and stir in the salt and pepper and keep for 5 minutes before serving.

Steak Quesadillas

Prep Time: 10 mins
Total Time: 25 mins

Servings per Recipe: 4
Calories   552 kcal
Fat   31.1 g
Carbohydrates   40g
Protein   28 g
Cholesterol   79 mg
Sodium   762 mg

Ingredients

2 tbsp vegetable oil, divided
1/2 onion, sliced
1/2 green bell pepper, sliced
salt to taste
4 flour tortillas

1/2 lb. cooked steak, cut into 1/4-inch thick pieces
1 C. shredded Mexican cheese blend

Directions

1. In a 10-inch skillet, heat 2 tsp of the oil on medium heat and sauté the onion and green bell pepper for about 5-10 minutes.
2. Stir in the salt and transfer the mixture into a bowl.
3. Brush 1 side of each tortilla with the remaining oil.
4. Place 1 tortilla, oil-side down, in the same skillet and sprinkle with 1/2 of the steak, 1/2 of the onion mixture and 1/2 of the Mexican cheese mixture.
5. Place a second tortilla, oil-side up, on top, pressing down with a spatula to seal.
6. Cook the quesadilla over medium heat for about 3-4 minutes per side.
7. Remove the quesadilla from skillet and cut into wedges.
8. Repeat with the remaining ingredients for second quesadilla.

THOUSAND ISLAND Ground Beef Quesadillas

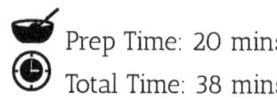

Prep Time: 20 mins
Total Time: 38 mins

Servings per Recipe: 4
Calories   521 kcal
Fat   30 g
Carbohydrates   38.4g
Protein   24.4 g
Cholesterol   79 mg
Sodium   777 mg

Ingredients

1/2 lb. ground beef
1/2 red onion, diced
1 clove garlic, minced
1 pinch salt
1 C. shredded Cheddar cheese, divided
1/4 C. shredded mozzarella cheese
1 tbsp milk

1 tbsp butter, divided
2 (12 inch) flour tortillas
2 tbsp Thousand Island dressing, divided
1 romaine lettuce heart, sliced
1 tomato, sliced
1/2 red onion, sliced

Directions

1. Heat a large skillet and cook the beef, diced onion and garlic for about 5-8 minutes.
2. Stir in the salt and transfer the beef mixture into a pan on low heat.
3. Add 3/4 C. of the Cheddar cheese, mozzarella cheese and milk and Cook, stirring for about 3-5 minutes.
4. In a large skillet, melt half of the butter on medium heat and cook 1 tortilla for about 3 minutes.
5. Flip the tortilla and spread 1 tbsp dressing over the tortilla evenly.
6. Place half of the beef mixture over the tortilla and fold in half.
7. Cook for about 1-2 minutes per side.
8. Transfer into a serving plate.
9. Repeat with second tortilla.
10. Sprinkle the remaining 1/4 C. of the Cheddar cheese over the tortillas.
11. Keep aside to cool for about 5 minutes.
12. Cut into the wedges and serve with the lettuce, tomato and sliced onion.

Vegetarian Quesadillas

Prep Time: 10 mins
Total Time: 40 mins

Servings per Recipe: 8
Calories	363 kcal
Fat	14.5 g
Carbohydrates	45.6 g
Protein	13.9 g
Cholesterol	26 mg
Sodium	732 mg

Ingredients

2 tsp olive oil
3 tbsp finely chopped onion
1 (15.5 oz.) can black beans, drained and rinsed
1 (10 oz.) can whole kernel corn, drained
1 tbsp brown sugar
1/4 C. salsa
1/4 tsp red pepper flakes
2 tbsp butter, divided
8 (8 inch) flour tortillas
1 1/2 C. shredded Monterey Jack cheese, divided

Directions

1. In a large pan, heat the oil on medium heat and sauté the onion for about 2 minutes.
2. Stir in the beans and corn, sugar, salsa and pepper flakes and cook for about 3 minutes.
3. In a large skillet, melt 2 tsp of the butter on medium heat.
4. Place a tortilla in the skillet and sprinkle with the cheese cheese and top with some of the bean mixture.
5. Place another tortilla on top and cook till golden brown from both sides.
6. Repeat with the remaining tortillas and filling.

SMOKY MUSHROOM
Quesadillas

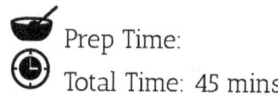

Prep Time:
Total Time: 45 mins

Servings per Recipe: 4
Calories	320 kcal
Fat	13.3 g
Carbohydrates	47.1g
Protein	12.4 g
Cholesterol	19 mg
Sodium	744 mg

Ingredients

1/2 C. prepared barbecue sauce
1 tbsp tomato paste
1 tbsp cider vinegar
1 chipotle chile in adobo sauce, minced
1 tbsp canola oil
1 lb. portobello mushroom caps, gills removed, diced
1 medium onion, finely diced
4 8- to 10-inch whole-wheat tortillas
3/4 C. shredded Monterey Jack cheese
2 tsp canola oil

Directions

1. In a bowl, mix together the barbecue sauce, tomato paste, vinegar and chipotle.
2. In a large nonstick skillet, heat 1 tbsp of the oil on medium heat and cook the mushrooms for about 5 minutes, stirring occasionally.,
3. Add the onion and cook for about 5-7 minutes.
4. Transfer the mushroom mixture into the bowl of the barbecue sauce and stir to combine.
5. Place the tortillas onto a smooth surface and spread 3 tbsp of the cheese on half of each tortilla and top with about 1/2 C. of the filling.
6. Fold the tortillas in half, pressing gently to flatten.
7. In a skillet, heat 1 tsp of the oil on medium heat and cook 2 quesadillas for about 3-4 minutes, turning once.
8. Transfer to a cutting board and tent with foil to keep warm.
9. Repeat with the remaining 1 tsp oil and quesadillas.
10. Cut each quesadilla into wedges and serve.

Little Tike
PB & J Quesadillas

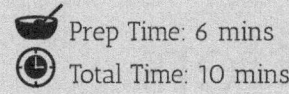

Prep Time: 6 mins
Total Time: 10 mins

Servings per Recipe: 2
Calories	276 kcal
Fat	13 g
Carbohydrates	34.7g
Protein	7.1 g
Cholesterol	5 mg
Sodium	318 mg

Ingredients

1 tsp butter
1 (10 inch) flour tortilla
2 tbsp peanut butter
2 tbsp grape jelly

Directions

1. In a skillet, melt the butter on medium heat.
2. Spread peanut butter over one side of the tortilla evenly.
3. Fold the tortilla in half, peanut butter is inside.
4. Place the tortilla in the skillet and cook for about 2 minutes from the both sides ,
5. Cut into wedges and dip in the jelly before serving.

PEAR
Fritters

Prep Time: 15 mins
Total Time: 30 mins

Servings per Recipe: 4
Calories 348 kcal
Fat 27.1 g
Carbohydrates 23.2g
Protein 4.3 g
Cholesterol 47 mg
Sodium 258 mg

Ingredients

1 tbsp olive oil
1 pear - peeled, cored and diced
2/3 C. all-purpose flour
1 tsp baking powder
1/4 tsp salt
1/8 tsp black pepper

1 egg
3 tbsp milk
oil for deep frying

Directions

1. In a skillet, heat oil on medium-high heat.
2. Add the pears and sauté till caramelized.
3. Remove from the heat and keep aside to cool.
4. Meanwhile, in a medium bowl mix together the flour, baking powder salt and pepper.
5. Make a well in the center of the flour mixture.
6. In another small bowl, add the egg and milk and beat well.
7. Add the egg mixture into the flour mixture and mix till well combined.
8. Gently fold in the pears.
9. Heat the oil in a deep fryer to 350 degrees F.
10. With a rounded spoonfuls, place the mixture into the hot oil and fry till golden brown.
11. Transfer onto a paper towel to drain.
12. Serve hot.

Summer Pear Salad

Prep Time: 20 mins
Total Time: 30 mins

Servings per Recipe: 6
Calories   426 kcal
Fat   31.6 g
Carbohydrates   33.1g
Protein   8 g
Cholesterol   21 mg
Sodium   654 mg

Ingredients

1 head leaf lettuce, torn into bite-size pieces
3 pears - peeled, cored and chopped
5 oz. Roquefort cheese, crumbled
1 avocado - peeled, pitted, and diced
1/2 C. thinly sliced green onions
1/4 C. white sugar
1/2 C. pecans

1/3 C. olive oil
3 tbsp red wine vinegar
1 1/2 tsp white sugar
1 1/2 tsp prepared mustard
1 clove garlic, chopped
1/2 tsp salt
fresh ground black pepper to taste

Directions

1. In a skillet, mix together 1/4 C. of the sugar and pecans on medium heat.
2. Cook, stirring gently till the sugar has melted and caramelized the pecans.
3. Transfer pecans onto a waxed paper and keep aside to cool.
4. Then break the pecans into pieces.
5. For the dressing in a bowl, add the oil, vinegar, 1 1/2 tsp of the sugar, mustard, chopped garlic, salt and pepper and beat till well combined.
6. In a large serving bowl, layer the lettuce, pears, blue cheese, avocado and green onions.
7. Pour the dressing over the salad and sprinkle with pecans and serve.

SWEET AND SOUR
Ground Beef

Prep Time: 10 mins
Total Time: 15 mins

Servings per Recipe: 6
Calories	233 kcal
Carbohydrates	5.1 g
Cholesterol	71 mg
Fat	14.4 g
Fiber	0.9 g
Protein	20.2 g
Sodium	356 mg

Ingredients

- 1 lb ground beef
- 1/4 cup yellow mustard
- 1 tbsp balsamic vinegar
- 1 tbsp minced garlic
- 1 1/2 tsps soy sauce
- 1 1/2 tsps honey
- 1 1/2 tsps paprika
- 1/8 tsp ground black pepper

Directions

1. Cook beef over medium heat in a skillet for about seven minutes or until brown before adding mustard, paprika, balsamic vinegar, garlic, soy sauce, honey, and black pepper, and cooking all this for another three minutes.
2. Serve.

Tijuana Ground Beef (Mexican Style)

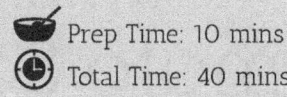 Prep Time: 10 mins
Total Time: 40 mins

Servings per Recipe: 4
Calories	732 kcal
Carbohydrates	52.1 g
Cholesterol	171 mg
Fat	43.7 g
Fiber	5.2 g
Protein	33.8 g
Sodium	592 mg

Ingredients

- 1 lb ground beef
- 1 cup salsa
- 1/2 cup water
- 1 green bell pepper, diced
- 1 bunch green onions, diced
- 1 (8 ounce) package wide egg noodles
- 1/2 cup sour cream
- 1/2 cup shredded Cheddar cheese
- 1 tomato, diced

Directions

1. Cook ground beef in a skillet until brown before stirring in water and salsa, and cooking all this for 10 minutes.
2. Now add onions and green pepper into the pan, and cook all this until you see that the veggies are tender before adding cooked noodles, grated cheese and sour cream.
3. Cover it up until the cheese melts before sprinkling some tomatoes.
4. Serve.

5-INGREDIENT
Tomato Sauce

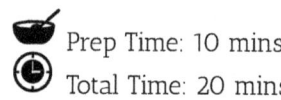
Prep Time: 10 mins
Total Time: 20 mins

Servings per Recipe: 4
Calories	70 kcal
Fat	3.1 g
Carbohydrates	6.6g
Protein	1.1 g
Cholesterol	8 mg
Sodium	188 mg

Ingredients

1/4 C. low-sodium canned chicken broth
1/4 C. dry vermouth or dry white wine
4 canned tomatoes, chopped
1/2 tsp minced fresh rosemary
1 tbsp butter

Directions

1. In a skillet, add all the ingredients except the butter and bring to a boil.
2. Cook till the liquid reduces to half.
3. Add the butter and immediately, stir till smooth.
4. Serve immediately with the steak.

Traditional Mexican Tomato Sauce

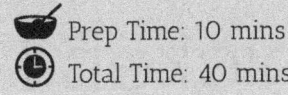

Prep Time: 10 mins
Total Time: 40 mins

Servings per Recipe: 10
Calories   17 kcal
Fat   0.2 g
Carbohydrates   3.8g
Protein   0.7 g
Cholesterol   0 mg
Sodium   36 mg

Ingredients

1 clove garlic, peeled
5 serrano peppers
1/2 onion, cut into 4 wedges

10 roma tomatoes
sea salt to taste

Directions

1. With a large piece of foil, cover a large skillet and heat on medium-high heat.
2. Add all the vegetables and roast the garlic for about 5 minutes, followed by 10 minutes for the onions and peppers and 15 minutes for the tomatoes.
3. Remove everything from the skillet and keep it aside to cool completely.
4. In a food processor, add the vegetables and salt and pulse till smooth.
5. Transfer the sauce into the airtight jars and preserve in the refrigerator for about 1 week.

CURRY
Chicken I

Prep Time: 10 mins
Total Time: 55 mins

Servings per Recipe: 4
Calories 210 kcal
Carbohydrates 6.2 g
Cholesterol 30 mg
Fat 15.4 g
Fiber 2 g
Protein 12.5 g
Sodium 322 mg

Ingredients

1/4 C. vegetable oil
1 onion, chopped
1 tomato, chopped
1 garlic clove, chopped
2 tbsps Jamaican-style curry powder, or normal curry powder
2 slices habanero pepper (optional)
1/4 tsp ground thyme
2 skinless, boneless chicken breast halves, cut into 1 1/2-inch pieces
1 C. water
1/2 tsp salt, or to taste

Directions

1. Get a frying pan. Get veggie oil hot.
2. Stir fry habaneros, onion, thyme, tomato, curry powder, and garlic for 7 mins. Add chicken and fry for 5 mins.
3. Add water to the onions and chicken, and set heat to low. Place a lid on pan. Let everything lightly boil for 30 mins.
4. Enjoy.

Skillet Marinara Sauce

Prep Time: 15 mins
Total Time: 1 hr 25 mins

Servings per Recipe: 6
Calories	147 kcal
Fat	7.4 g
Carbohydrates	16.5 g
Protein	2.7 g
Cholesterol	0 mg
Sodium	403 mg

Ingredients

- 3 tbsp olive oil
- 1/2 onion, chopped
- 8 large tomatoes, peeled and cut into big chunks
- 6 cloves garlic, minced
- 1 bay leaf
- 1/2 C. red wine
- 1 tbsp honey
- 2 tsp dried basil
- 1 tsp oregano
- 1 tsp dried marjoram
- 1 tsp salt
- 1/2 tsp ground black pepper
- 1/4 tsp fennel seed
- 1/4 tsp crushed red pepper
- 2 tsp balsamic vinegar

Directions

1. In a pan, heat the oil on medium heat and sauté the onion for about 5 minutes.
2. Add the tomatoes, bay leaf and garlic and bring to a boil.
3. Reduce the heat to medium-low and simmer for about 30 minutes.
4. Stir in the remaining ingredients except vinegar and again bring to a gentle simmer.
5. Simmer for about 30 minutes.
6. Remove everything from the heat and immediately, stir in the vinegar.

MALAYSIAN
Mango Chicken

Prep Time: 20 mins
Total Time: 30 mins

Servings per Recipe: 4
Calories 312 kcal
Fat 5.4 g
Cholesterol 36.4g
Sodium 29.2 g
Carbohydrates 68 mg
Protein 81 mg

Ingredients

4 skinless, boneless chicken breasts
3/4 C. chopped red onion
1 mango - peeled, seeded, and sliced
1 tbsp vegetable oil

3 C. orange juice
3 tbsp cornstarch
1/4 C. hot water

Directions

1. Heat a large skillet and cook the chicken till browned completely.
2. Add the red onion and cook, stirring occasionally for about 2-3 minutes.
3. Stir in the orange juice and bring to a boil.
4. Stir in the mango slices and reduce the heat, then simmer for about 2 minutes.
5. Meanwhile in a bowl, mix together the hot water and cornstarch.
6. Add the cornstarch mixture in the pan and cook, stirring till the mixture becomes thick.

Vegetarian Mango Curry Indian Style

Prep Time: 25 mins
Total Time: 45 mins

Servings per Recipe: 4
Calories   323 kcal
Fat   21.6 g
Carbohydrates   19.1g
Protein   17.7 g
Cholesterol   0 mg
Sodium   175 mg

Ingredients

- 1 tbsp sesame oil
- 5 cloves garlic, minced
- 1 tbsp minced ginger
- 1 firm mango, peeled and sliced
- 3 tbsp yellow curry powder
- 2 tbsp chopped cilantro
- 1 (14 oz.) can light coconut milk
- 1 (14 oz.) package extra firm tofu, cubed
- 1/4 tsp salt and pepper to taste

Directions

1. In a large skillet, heat the oil on medium-high heat and sauté the ginger and garlic for about 1-2 minutes.
2. Add the mango and cook for about 1 minute.
3. Stir in the cilantro and curry powder and cook for about 1 minute.
4. Stir in the coconut milk and bring to a simmer.
5. Stir in the tofu, salt and black pepper and simmer, stirring occasionally for about 5 minutes.

MALAYSIAN
Mango Chicken

Prep Time: 20 mins
Total Time: 30 mins

Servings per Recipe: 4
Calories   312 kcal
Fat   5.4 g
Cholesterol   36.4g
Sodium   29.2 g
Carbohydrates   68 mg
Protein   81 mg

Ingredients

4 skinless, boneless chicken breasts
3/4 C. chopped red onion
1 mango - peeled, seeded, and sliced
1 tbsp vegetable oil

3 C. orange juice
3 tbsp cornstarch
1/4 C. hot water

Directions

1. Heat a large skillet and cook the chicken till browned completely.
2. Add the red onion and cook, stirring occasionally for about 2-3 minutes.
3. Stir in the orange juice and bring to a boil.
4. Stir in the mango slices and reduce the heat, then simmer for about 2 minutes.
5. Meanwhile in a bowl, mix together the hot water and cornstarch.
6. Add the cornstarch mixture in the pan and cook, stirring till the mixture becomes thick.

Hot Italian Skillet Pizza

Prep Time: 15 mins
Total Time: 40 mins

Servings per Recipe: 2
Calories	323 kcal
Fat	25.2 g
Carbohydrates	13.2g
Protein	11.7 g
Cholesterol	46 mg
Sodium	554 mg

Ingredients

- 1 tbsp olive oil
- 1 Spanish onion, thinly sliced
- 1 green bell pepper, thinly sliced
- 1 (3.5 oz.) link hot Italian sausage, sliced
- 1/4 C. sliced fresh mushrooms, or more to taste
- 1 slice prepared polenta, cut into 4x4-inch piece
- 1/4 C. spaghetti sauce, or as needed
- 1 oz. shredded mozzarella cheese

Directions

1. In a large skillet, heat the oil on medium heat and sauté the sausage, bell pepper, mushrooms and onion for about 10-15 minutes.
2. Transfer the mixture into a large bowl.
3. In the same skillet, add the polenta and cook for about 5 minutes on both sides.
4. Top the polenta with the sausage mixture, followed by the spaghetti sauce and mozzarella cheese.
5. Cook for about 5-10 minutes.

PAELLA
in Mediterranean Style

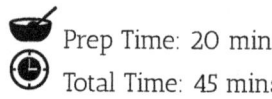
Prep Time: 20 mins
Total Time: 45 mins

Servings per Recipe: 4
Calories 484.3
Cholesterol 52.5mg
Sodium 1207.2mg
Carbohydrates 51.1g
Protein 26.6g

Ingredients

3 tbsp olive oil
1 medium onion, chopped
2 tbsp fresh minced garlic
1 tsp dried chili pepper flakes
1 small red bell pepper, seeded and chopped
1 C. frozen artichoke heart, thawed
3/4 C. sliced pitted olive
1 (14 oz.) cans chicken broth
1 C. water

1 C. uncooked long-grain white rice
salt, to taste
1/2 tsp paprika
1 pinch saffron thread
black pepper
2 C. cooked chicken, chopped
3/4 C. frozen green pea, thawed

Directions

1. In a large skillet, heat the oil on medium heat and sauté the onion, bell pepper, garlic and chili flakes for about 3 minutes.
2. Stir in the olives and artichokes and sauté for about 2 minutes.
3. Add the water and broth and bring to a boil.
4. Reduce the heat to medium-low and simmer, covered for about 15 minutes.
5. Stir in the chicken and peas and simmer, covered for about 5-7 minutes.
6. Remove everything from the heat and keep aside, covered for about 5 minutes before serving.

Argentinian Tomato and Corn Chicken

Prep Time: 30 mins
Total Time: 1 hr 30 mins

Servings per Recipe: 8
Calories   476 kcal
Fat   10.5 g
Carbohydrates   40.5g
Protein   56.6 g
Cholesterol   137 mg
Sodium   1003 mg

Ingredients

8 bone-in chicken breast halves, with skin
1 C. all-purpose flour
1 tbsp vegetable oil
2 (15 oz.) cans tomato sauce
2 (15 oz.) cans whole kernel corn
1/2 C. diced onion
2 cloves garlic, minced
2 tbsp chili powder
1/2 tsp crushed red pepper flakes
salt to taste

Directions

1. Roll the chicken breast halves in the flour evenly.
2. In a large skillet, heat the oil and cook the chicken for about 5-7 minutes.
3. Remove everything from the heat and keep it aside.
4. In a pan, mix together the onion, corn and tomato sauce and bring to a boil.
5. Stir in the chicken and the remaining ingredients and reduce the heat to low.
6. Simmer for about 1 hour.

LOUISIANA
Shrimp

Prep Time: 5 mins
Total Time: 15 mins

Servings per Recipe: 4
Calories   166 kcal
Carbohydrates   0.9 g
Cholesterol   259 mg
Fat   5 g
Fiber   0.5 g
Protein   28 g
Sodium   443 mg

Ingredients

- 1 tsp paprika
- 3/4 tsp dried thyme
- 3/4 tsp dried oregano
- 1/4 tsp garlic powder
- 1/4 tsp salt
- 1/4 tsp ground black pepper
- 1/4 tsp cayenne pepper, or more to taste
- 1 1/2 pounds large shrimp, peeled and deveined
- 1 tbsp vegetable oil

Directions

1. Coat shrimp with the mixture of paprika, garlic powder, thyme, oregano, salt, pepper, and cayenne pepper in a sealable plastic bag.
2. Now cook this shrimp in the hot oil in a skillet for about four minutes or until you see that it is no longer transparent from the center.
3. Serve.

Classical American Style Fried Chicken Cutlets

Prep Time: 20 mins
Total Time: 35 mins

Servings per Recipe: 4
Calories   391 kcal
Fat   11.4 g
Carbohydrates   37.3g
Protein   32.8 g
Cholesterol   116 mg
Sodium   935 mg

Ingredients

- 2 tsp garlic powder
- 1 tsp ground black pepper
- 1 tsp salt
- 1 tsp paprika
- 1/2 C. seasoned bread crumbs
- 1 C. all-purpose flour
- 1/2 C. milk
- 1 egg
- 4 skinless, boneless chicken breast halves
- 1 C. oil for frying, or as needed

Directions

1. In a shallow dish, add the egg and milk and beat well.
2. In another shallow dish mix together the flour, breadcrumbs, garlic powder, paprika, salt and black pepper.
3. Get your oil, in a skillet to 350 degrees F.
4. Dip the chicken breast halves in the egg mixture and then roll in the flour mixture evenly.
5. Fry the chicken breast halves for about 10 minutes, flipping once half way.
6. Serve hot.

CRISPY PAPRIKA Chicken

Prep Time: 20 mins
Total Time: 50 mins

Servings per Recipe: 8
Calories	489 kcal
Fat	21.8 g
Carbohydrates	29.5g
Protein	40.7 g
Cholesterol	116 mg
Sodium	140 mg

Ingredients

- 1 (4 lb.) chicken, cut into pieces
- 1 C. buttermilk
- 2 C. all-purpose flour for coating
- 1 tsp paprika
- salt and pepper to taste
- 2 quarts vegetable oil for frying

Directions

1. In a shallow dish, place the buttermilk.
2. In another shallow dish, place the flour, salt, black pepper and paprika.
3. Dip the chicken pieces in the buttermilk completely and coat them in the flour mixture.
4. Arrange the chicken pieces on a baking dish and cover with wax paper and keep aside till flour becomes pasty.
5. In a large cast iron skillet, heat the vegetable oil and fry the chicken pieces till browned.
6. Reduce the heat and cook, covered for about 30 minutes.
7. Uncover and increase the heat and cook till crispy.
8. Transfer the chicken pieces onto paper towel lined plates to drain..

Elegant Apple & Cheddar Stuffed Chicken Breast

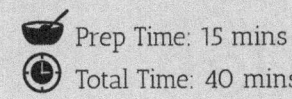

Prep Time: 15 mins
Total Time: 40 mins

Servings per Recipe: 4
Calories	139 kcal
Fat	5.1 g
Carbohydrates	4.9 g
Protein	15 g
Cholesterol	46 mg
Sodium	120 mg

Ingredients

- 2 skinless, boneless chicken breasts
- 1/2 C. chopped apple
- 2 tbsp shredded Cheddar cheese
- 1 tbsp Italian-style dried bread crumbs
- 1 tbsp butter
- 1/4 C. dry white wine
- 1/4 C. water
- 1 tbsp water
- 1 1/2 tsp cornstarch
- 1 tbsp chopped fresh parsley, for garnish

Directions

1. In a bowl, mix together the apple, breadcrumbs and cheese.
2. Place the chicken breasts between 2 sheets of wax paper and with a meat mallet, flatten to 1/4-inch thickness.
3. Place the mixture in the center of the chicken breasts evenly.
4. Roll each breast around the filling and secure with the toothpicks.
5. In a large skillet, melt the butter on medium heat and cook the chicken breasts till browned completely.
6. Add the wine and 1/4 C. of the water and simmer, covered for about 15-20 mins.
7. Transfer the chicken breasts onto a plate.
8. In a bowl, mix together the cornstarch and the remaining water.
9. Add the cornstarch mixture in the skillet with juices and cook till the gravy becomes thick.
10. Pour the gravy over the chicken breasts and serve with a garnishing of parsley.

CREAMY MUSHROOM
Skillet

🥣 Prep Time: 15 mins
🕐 Total Time: 45 mins

Servings per Recipe: 6
Calories 329
Fat 17.6g
Cholesterol 61mg
Sodium 338mg
Carbohydrates 13.6g
Fiber 3.6g
Protein 7.7g

Ingredients

4 bacon strips, chopped
1 (16 oz.) package frozen green peas, thawed
½ C. red onion, chopped
1 C. heavy whipping cream
Drop of Worcestershire sauce
Pinch of monosodium glutamate
Pinch of salt and freshly ground black pepper
1 (14 oz.) package fresh mushrooms, sliced
2 tsp cooking sherry

Directions

1. Heat a large nonstick skillet on medium-high heat.
2. Add bacon and cook for about 8-10 mins or till crisp.
3. Meanwhile in a pan of boiling water, add peas and cook for about 5-7 mins. Drain well.
4. Add onion in the skillet with bacon and cook for about 5-7 mins.
5. Stir in cream and cook for about 5 mins.
6. Stir in Worcestershire sauce, monosodium glutamate, salt and black pepper.
7. Now, stir in mushrooms, peas and sherry and gently, stir to coat with bacon mixture.
8. Serve hot.

Hearty Simple Burger

Prep Time: 5 mins
Total Time: 20 mins

Servings per Recipe: 8
Calories	229 kcal
Carbohydrates	3.5 g
Cholesterol	82 mg
Fat	18.2 g
Fiber	0.2 g
Protein	12.1 g
Sodium	247 mg

Ingredients

- 1 lb ground beef
- 1 slice bread, crumbled
- 1 egg
- 2 tbsps prepared mustard
- 3 tbsps Worcestershire sauce
- garlic salt to taste
- salt and pepper to taste

Directions

1. Take out a large bowl and mix beef, egg, Worcestershire sauce and mustard.
2. Now make 8 patties and also add some salt, pepper and garlic (salt according to your taste).
3. Now cook these patties in a skillet that is over medium heat for about 15 mins to reach the required tenderness.

NEW ENGLAND
Fried Chips and Fried Fish

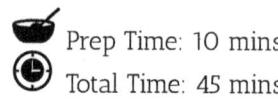

Prep Time: 10 mins
Total Time: 45 mins

Servings per Recipe: 4
Calories   782 kcal
Fat   26.2 g
Carbohydrates   91.9 g
Protein   44.6 g
Cholesterol   125 mg
Sodium   861 mg

Ingredients

1 C. all-purpose flour
1 tsp baking powder
Salt and freshly ground black pepper, to taste
1 egg, beaten lightly
1 C. milk
4 large potatoes, peeled and cut into strips lengthwise
4 C. vegetable oil
1 1/2 lbs cod fillets

Directions

1. In a large bowl, add flour, baking powder, salt, black pepper, egg and milk.
2. Mix till well combined.
3. Keep everything aside for at least 20 minutes.
4. In a large bowl of chilled water, dip the potatoes for 2-3 minutes.
5. Drain the mix well and pat dry with paper towel.
6. In a large skillet, heat the oil with medium heat.
7. Add the potatoes and fry for about 3-4 minutes or till crisp and tender.
8. Transfer the potatoes onto a paper towel lined plate.
9. Coat the cod fillets in the flour mixture evenly.
10. Fry everything for about 3-4 minutes or till golden brown.
11. Transfer the cod fillets onto another paper towel lined plate.
12. Now, return the potato strips to the skillet and fry them for about 1-2 minutes more or till crispy.

Szechwan Shrimp

🥣 Prep Time: 10 mins
🕐 Total Time: 20 mins

Servings per Recipe: 4
Carbohydrates 6.7 g
Cholesterol 164 mg
Fat 4.4 g
Fiber 0.4 g
Protein 18.3 g
Sodium 500 mg

Ingredients

4 tbsps water
2 tbsps ketchup
1 tbsp soy sauce
2 tsps cornstarch
1 tsp honey
1/2 tsp crushed red pepper
1/4 tsp ground ginger

1 tbsp vegetable oil
1/4 cup sliced green onions
4 cloves garlic, minced
12 ounces cooked shrimp, tails removed

Directions

1. Combine water, crushed red pepper, ketchup, soy sauce, cornstarch, honey and ground ginger in a medium sized bowl and set it aside.
2. Cook green onions and garlic in hot oil for about 30 seconds before adding shrimp and mixing it well.
3. Now add sauce and cook until you see that the sauce has thickened.
4. Serve.

CHICKEN BREASTS
With Chipotle Gravy

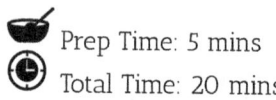
Prep Time: 5 mins
Total Time: 20 mins

Servings per Recipe: 2
Calories   333 kcal
Fat   22.2 g
Carbohydrates   4.1g
Protein   28.3 g
Cholesterol   104 mg
Sodium   188 mg

Ingredients

2 skinless, boneless chicken breast halves
salt and fresh ground pepper to taste
1 tbsp olive oil
2 tbsps butter
1 tbsp all-purpose flour
3/4 C. chicken broth
2 tbsps minced green onions
1/2 tsp chipotle chili powder, or more to taste

Directions

1. With a meat mallet, pound the chicken breast halves into 1/2-inch thickness by it placing between 2 heavy plastic sheets.
2. In a skillet, heat the oil till it begins to simmer on high heat.
3. Reduce the heat to medium and add the chicken breasts and sprinkle with salt and black pepper.
4. Cook the chicken for about 5 minutes on both sides or till browned.
5. Place the breasts into a plate covered with foil to keep them warm.
6. In the same skillet melt the butter and cook the flour stirring continuously for about 2 minutes.
7. Add the broth and cook, scraping the brown bits for about 1-2 minutes.
8. Stir in the chicken, chipotle powder and green onion and cook for about 1-2 minutes.

Banana & Brown Sugar Spring Rolls

Prep Time: 10 mins
Total Time: 20 mins

Servings per Recipe: 8
Calories   325 kcal
Fat   11.6 g
Carbohydrates   53.3g
Protein   3.5 g
Cholesterol   3 mg
Sodium   191 mg

Ingredients

2 large bananas
8 (7 inch square) spring roll wrappers
1 C. brown sugar, or to taste
1 quart oil for deep frying

Directions

1. In a large cast-iron skillet or deep fryer, heat the oil to 375 degrees F.
2. Slice the bananas in half lengthwise and cut into fourths crosswise.
3. Arrange 1 piece of banana over the corner of a spring roll wrapper diagonally and sprinkle with brown sugar.
4. Roll the each corner of the wrapper to the center and fold bottom and top corners in and continue rolling.
5. With your wet fingers brush the edges of the wrapper to seal the roll.
6. Carefully, add the banana rolls in the skillet in batches.
7. Fry the rolls till golden brown and transfer onto paper towel lined plates to drain.

BED AND BREAKFAST
Pancakes

Prep Time: 10 mins
Total Time: 25 mins

Servings per Recipe: 4
Calories	353 kcal
Fat	10 g
Carbohydrates	58.5g
Protein	7.7 g
Cholesterol	51 mg
Sodium	517 mg

Ingredients

1 egg
2 tablespoons vegetable oil
1 cup milk
1 cup all-purpose flour
1/2 teaspoon baking soda
1/2 teaspoon salt
1/2 cup light brown sugar
1 packet instant, banana-flavored oatmeal

Directions

1. Get a bowl, combine: milk, oil, and egg.
2. Get a 2nd bowl, combine: oatmeal, flour, brown sugar, baking soda, and salt.
3. Combine both bowls evenly then begin to get a skillet hot with oil.
4. Once the oil is hot ladle some of the batter onto the pan and fry one side until it is golden for 4 mins then flip it and continue to fry the opposite side.
5. Enjoy.

Skillet Buttery Bananas

Prep Time: 10 mins
Total Time: 15 mins

Servings per Recipe: 6
Calories	169 kcal
Fat	6 g
Carbohydrates	30.5g
Protein	0.7 g
Cholesterol	15 mg
Sodium	42 mg

Ingredients

3 firm bananas, halved lengthwise
1/2 cup white sugar
1 1/4 teaspoons ground cinnamon
3 tablespoons butter

Directions

1. Slice your banana into two pieces, then cut each half into 4 additional pieces.
2. Get a bowl combine: cinnamon and sugar.
3. Get your butter hot in a frying pan then layer in the banana and fry them for 7 mins.
4. Flip the bananas half way.
5. When serving the bananas coat them with some of the sugar mix.
6. Enjoy

CABBAGE & CARROT
Spring Rolls

Prep Time: 30 mins
Total Time: 45 mins

Servings per Recipe: 20
Calories 47.2
Cholesterol 0.7mg
Sodium 81.8mg
Carbohydrates 8.2g
Protein 1.5g

Ingredients

1 tbsp peanut oil
2 green onions, chopped
2 garlic cloves, minced
2 carrots, peeled and chopped finely
1 head green cabbage, cored and chopped
2 tbsps stir-fry sauce

1/8 tsp cayenne pepper
1/4 tsp freshly ground white pepper
2 tbsps rice wine
20-25 spring roll wrappers
Oil, as required

Directions

1. In a large skillet, heat peanut oil on medium heat and sauté green onion, garlic and carrot for about 5 minutes.
2. Add cabbage, stir-fry sauce and both peppers and cook for about 15 minutes.
3. Stir in the wine and cook till just absorbed.
4. Remove everything from the heat and keep aside to cool completely.
5. Place the wrappers onto a smooth surface.
6. Divide the veggie mixture in the center of each wrapper evenly.
7. Fold the inner sides of the wrappers around the filling and roll tightly.
8. In a large cast-iron skillet or deep fryer, heat the oil.
9. Carefully, add the rolls in the skillet in batches.
10. Fry the rolls till golden brown and transfer onto paper towel lined plates to drain.

Spicy Beef Spring Rolls

Prep Time: 5 mins
Total Time: 15 mins

Servings per Recipe: 20
Calories   177.9
Cholesterol   16.5mg
Sodium   401.6mg
Carbohydrates   15.9g
Protein   7.7g

Ingredients

2 tbsps olive oil
1 medium onion, chopped
1 lb lean ground beef
1 tbsp fresh ginger, minced
3 garlic cloves, minced
1 tsp chili paste
1/4 C. soy sauce
Salt and freshly ground black pepper, to taste
1 head green cabbage, cored and shredded
2 medium carrots, peeled and grated
3 scallions, slice thinly
1 tbsp fresh lime juice
1 (14-oz.) package spring roll wrappers
1/2 C. oil

Directions

1. In a large skillet, heat olive oil and sauté onion till tender.
2. Add beef and cook for about 1-2 minutes.
3. Add ginger, garlic, chili paste, soy sauce, salt and black pepper and cook for about 10-15 minutes.
4. Add cabbage and cook for about 5-10 minutes.
5. Stir in the carrots and stir fry till all the liquid is absorbed.
6. Stir in the scallion and lemon juice and stir fry for about 1 minute and Remove everything from the heat to cool.
7. Place the wrappers onto a smooth surface.
8. Divide the beef mixture in the center of each wrapper evenly.
9. Roll the wrappers around the filling and with your wet fingers brush the edges and press to seal completely.
10. In a large cast-iron skillet, heat the oil.
11. Carefully, add the rolls to the skillet in batches.
12. Fry the rolls till golden brown and transfer onto paper towel lined plates to drain.

A JAPANESE
Stir-Fry

⏲ Prep Time: 30 mins
⏱ Total Time: 45 mins

Servings per Recipe: 8
Calories	290 kcal
Carbohydrates	26.4 g
Cholesterol	39 mg
Fat	7.6 g
Fiber	2.6 g
Protein	26.4 g
Sodium	1271 mg

Ingredients

2 pounds boneless beef sirloin or beef top round steaks (3/4" thick)
3 tbsps cornstarch
1 (10.5 ounce) can Campbell's® Condensed Beef Broth
1/2 cup soy sauce
2 tbsps sugar
2 tbsps vegetable oil
4 cups sliced shiitake mushrooms
1 head Chinese cabbage (bok choy), thinly sliced
2 medium red peppers, cut into 2"-long strips
3 stalks celery, sliced
2 medium green onions, cut into 2" pieces
Hot cooked regular long-grain white rice

Directions

1. To start this recipe grab a knife and begin to cut your beef into some thin long strips.
2. Grab a medium sized bowl and combine the following ingredients: sugar, broth, soy, and cornstarch.
3. After combining the ingredients let the contents rest for a bit.
4. Get your wok hot over a high level of heat and add one 1 tbsp of oil to it. Allow the oil to heat up as well.
5. Once your oil is hot combine the following ingredients in it: green onions, mushrooms, celery, cabbage, and peppers.
6. Fry these veggies down until you find that they are soft. Once soft remove them from the heat.
7. Now grab your cornstarch mixture and put it in the pot fry and continually stir until you find that it has thicken.
8. Once thick combine the cornstarch with your beef and veggies. Fry until beef is cooked completely.
9. Let contents cool. Enjoy.

The Best Chicken Stir-Fry I Know

Prep Time: 30 mins
Total Time: 1 hr 20 mins

Servings per Recipe: 6
Calories   700 kcal
Carbohydrates   76.7 g
Cholesterol   161 mg
Fat   12.1 g
Fiber   4.9 g
Protein   67.7 g
Sodium   1790 mg

Ingredients

- 2 cups white rice
- 4 cups water
- 2/3 cup soy sauce
- 1/4 cup brown sugar
- 1 tbsp cornstarch
- 1 tbsp minced fresh ginger
- 1 tbsp minced garlic
- 1/4 tsp red pepper flakes
- 3 skinless, boneless chicken breast halves, thinly sliced
- 1 tbsp sesame oil
- 1 green bell pepper, cut into matchsticks
- 1 (8 ounce) can sliced water chestnuts, drained
- 1 head broccoli, broken into florets
- 1 cup sliced carrots
- 1 onion, cut into large chunks
- 1 tbsp sesame oil

Directions

1. Get a saucepan. Add rice and water. Get water boiling with high heat. Once boiling lower heat to low. Cover and let rice cook for 25 to 30 mins.
2. Get a small bowl and mix the following ingredients: corn starch, soy sauce, and brown sugar.
3. Combine with the corn starch: red pepper, ginger, and garlic.
4. This is your marinade. Cover chicken with it for 30 mins.
5. Get a wok heat 1 tbsp of sesame oil hot with high heat.
6. Fry the following ingredients for 6 mins: onion, bell pepper, carrots, water chestnuts, and broccoli. Place aside.
7. Add 1 tbsp of sesame oil to your frying pan and get it hot.
8. Grab your chicken and separate the meat and marinade.
9. Fry the chicken for 3 mins on each side until almost cooked but not 100% done.
10. Add veggies to the chicken and stir fry everything for 10 mins.
11. Enjoy.

BEEF
Stir-Fry I

Prep Time: 10 mins
Total Time: 1 hr 10 mins

Servings per Recipe: 4
Calories	665 kcal
Carbohydrates	104.6 g
Cholesterol	39 mg
Fat	13.8 g
Fiber	11.7 g
Protein	30.5 g
Sodium	1594 mg

Ingredients

2 cups brown rice
4 cups water
2 tbsps cornstarch
2 tsps white sugar
6 tbsps soy sauce
1/4 cup white wine
1 tbsp minced fresh ginger
1 pound boneless beef round steak, cut into thin strips
1 tbsp vegetable oil
3 cups broccoli florets
2 carrots, thinly sliced
1 (6 ounce) package frozen pea pods, thawed
2 tbsps chopped onion
1 (8 ounce) can sliced water chestnuts, undrained
1 cup Chinese cabbage
2 large heads bok choy, chopped
1 tbsp vegetable oil

Directions

1. Get a large pan. Add water, heat until boiling. Add rice. Lower heat to low. Cover the pan. Let the rice cook for 40 mins until done.
2. Get a bowl combine the following ingredients: soy sauce, cornstarch, wine, and sugar. Mix evenly then add ginger. Add beef to this marinade.
3. Get wok. Heat 1 tsp oil for frying. Stir fry for 1 min: onions, broccoli, pea pods, and carrots.
4. Mix in: bok choy, Chinese cabbage, and water chestnuts. Place a lid on the pan and let fry for 4 mins.
5. Remove everything from pan.
6. Add 1 tsp oil to pan and fry beef for 4 mins. Add veggies back and fry for 3 mins.
7. Enjoy with rice.

Orange-Chicken Stir Fry

🥣 Prep Time: 15 mins
⏱ Total Time: 1 hr

Servings per Recipe: 4
Calories   849 kcal
Carbohydrates   112.5 g
Cholesterol   129 mg
Fat   17.5 g
Fiber   15.7 g
Protein   67.6 g
Sodium   1838 mg

Ingredients

1 (16 ounce) package dry whole-wheat noodles
1/2 cup chicken stock
1/2 cup orange marmalade
1/3 cup tamari sauce
1 (1 inch) piece ginger root, peeled
ground black pepper to taste
1 lemon, juiced
3 tbsps peanut oil
2 pounds skinless, boneless chicken breast halves, cut into thin strips
1 (16 ounce) bag frozen stir-fry vegetables, thawed

Directions

1. Get a pan. Add water and salt. Heat until boiling. Add wheat noodles. Boil for 8 mins. Drain and set aside.
2. Get a wok. Add following ingredients fry until sauce thickens: ground black pepper, chicken stock, ginger root piece, tamari sauce, and orange marmalade. Use low heat. Should take 20 mins. Set aside add lemon juice.
3. Heat peanut oil in wok. Fry chicken for 6 - 10 mins. Set aside.
4. Fry veggies for 5 mins. Add chicken, add sauce. Fry for 2 mins. Remove ginger root.
5. Let the contents cool. Serve with your noodles.
6. Enjoy.

TURKEY
Stir-Fry

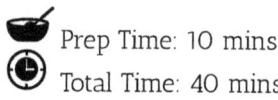
Prep Time: 10 mins
Total Time: 40 mins

Servings per Recipe: 4
Calories   294 kcal
Carbohydrates   22.2 g
Cholesterol   67 mg
Fat   11.7 g
Fiber   2.7 g
Protein   25.5 g
Sodium   403 mg

Ingredients

- 1 pound turkey meat, diced
- 2 tbsps oyster sauce, divided
- 1 (1 inch) piece fresh ginger root, finely chopped, divided
- 2 tbsps Chinese cooking wine, divided
- 1 tbsp vegetable oil
- 1 tbsp minced garlic
- 1 (11 ounce) can lychees, drained
- 2 red chile peppers, seeded and sliced into strips
- 1 tbsp soy sauce, or to taste
- 1 dash ground black pepper
- 1 bunch fresh cilantro, chopped
- 1 bunch green onions, chopped

Directions

1. Get bowl and combine the following: 1 tbsp of Chinese cooking wine, 1 table of oyster sauce, and half of your ginger. Use this to marinate your turkey for at least twenty mins.
2. Get a frying pan and heat oil. Add garlic and let it fry until golden.
3. Add your turkey with marinade and combine wine and ginger mix plus your oyster sauce, soy sauce, chili peppers, and lychees and cook for 5 mins.
4. Add some fresh cilantro, peppers, and green onions before serving.
5. Enjoy.

Tofu Stir Fry II

Prep Time: 15 mins
Total Time: 45 mins

Servings per Recipe: 2
Calories   167 kcal
Fat   7.7 g
Carbohydrates   21.2g
Protein   4.6 g
Cholesterol   0 mg
Sodium   216 mg

Ingredients

- 1/3 cup lite soy sauce
- 1 tbsp Thai garlic chili paste
- 2 cloves garlic, diced
- 2 tsps cayenne pepper
- 1 1/2 tsps diced fresh ginger
- 1/2 (16 ounce) package linguine-style rice noodles
- 3 tbsps olive oil
- 1 (12 ounce) package extra-firm tofu, cut into 1/2-inch cubes
- 3 green onions, minced
- 1 cup snow peas
- 1/2 green bell pepper, sliced
- 1/2 red bell pepper, sliced

Directions

1. Get a bowl combine the following: ginger, soy sauce, cayenne pepper, garlic chili paste, and garlic.
2. Get another bowl and fill it with hot water put your noodles in this water let it sit covered for 10 mins until soft. After 10 mins drain them.
3. Grab your frying pan and with medium heat get oil hot.
4. Stir fry tofu cubes until golden (6 mins). Combine green onion and fry for another 2 mins.
5. Now put one half of the wet mixture over the tofu get it simmering for 5 mins.
6. Mix in green bell pepper, snow peas, and red bell pepper and stir fry until veggies are soft. 5 mins.
7. Add the other half of the wet mixture and cook until the mixture is very thick and your veggies are tender but not too soft. About 5 mins.
8. Mix in your noodles and get everything evenly coated. Stir frying for 3 to 5 mins.
9. Let the contents cool.
10. Enjoy.

CHICKEN and Garlic

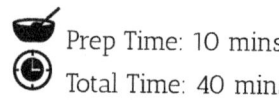
Prep Time: 10 mins
Total Time: 40 mins

Servings per Recipe: 4
Calories 337 kcal
Fat 8.6 g
Carbohydrates 32.3g
Protein 31.7 g
Cholesterol 67 mg
Sodium 1364 mg

Ingredients

- 2 tbsps peanut oil
- 6 cloves garlic, minced
- 1 tsp grated fresh ginger
- 1 bunch green onions, diced
- 1 tsp salt
- 1 lb boneless skinless chicken breasts, cut into strips
- 2 onions, thinly sliced
- 1 C. sliced cabbage
- 1 red bell pepper, thinly sliced
- 2 C. sugar snap peas
- 1 C. chicken broth
- 2 tbsps soy sauce
- 2 tbsps white sugar
- 2 tbsps cornstarch

Directions

1. Get your peanut oil hot. Then add in: salt, 2 pieces of garlic, green onions, and ginger root.
2. Cook this mix for 4 mins then add the chicken and cook everything for 4 more mins.
3. Combine 1/2 C. broth, the rest of the garlic, peas, sweet onions, bell peppers, and cabbage. Then place a lid on the pot.
4. Get a bowl, combine: cornstarch, 1/2 C. broth, sugar, and soy sauce.
5. Pour this into the cabbage mix and stir the contents to coat all the ingredients.
6. Cook this mix for 2 more mins then serve.
7. Enjoy.

Lemon and Shrimp Stir Fry (Paleo Approved)

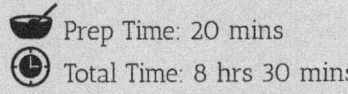

Prep Time: 20 mins
Total Time: 8 hrs 30 mins

Servings per Recipe: 4	
Calories	388 kcal
Fat	31.7 g
Carbohydrates	5.9 g
Protein	21.1 g
Cholesterol	192 mg
Sodium	222 mg

Ingredients

- 1/2 C. lemon juice
- 1 small onion, finely diced
- 1/2 C. olive oil
- 3 cloves garlic, minced
- 1 tbsp lemon zest
- 1 tbsp grated ginger
- 1 tsp ground turmeric
- 24 large shrimp, peeled and deveined
- 1 tbsp coconut oil, or as needed

Directions

1. Get a bowl, combine: turmeric, lemon juice, ginger, onion, lemon zest, garlic, and olive oil.
2. Add in the shrimp and stir the contents.
3. Now place a covering of plastic on the bowl and put everything in the fridge for 8 hrs.
4. Separate the shrimp from the marinade and reserve the liquid.
5. Now get your wok hot with coconut oil.
6. Add in the shrimp and cook the mix for 7 mins then add in the marinade and get everything boiling while stirring.
7. Once the mix has boiled for 60 secs serve it.
8. Enjoy.

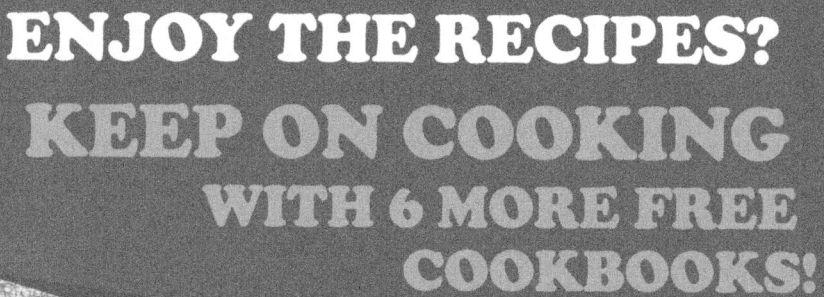

ENJOY THE RECIPES?
KEEP ON COOKING WITH 6 MORE FREE COOKBOOKS!

Click the link below and simply enter your email address to join the club and receive your 6 cookbooks.

http://booksumo.com/magnet

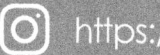 https://www.instagram.com/booksumopress/

 https://www.facebook.com/booksumo/

Made in the USA
Monee, IL
19 December 2019